Hiya friends, this is Bo!
He takes his blanket
wherever he goes.

He can pull it fast,
or he can drag it slow.

Through the grass,
or through the snow.

The cars all see him,
and they start to slow.
Once they stop,
Joe yells,
"GO BO, GO!"

Bo crosses the street,
blanket in tow,
with a wag of his tail,
he says, "Hiya Joe!"

After some pets,
he says bye to Joe.
He continues his journey,
with two hops in a row.

There's a tree in the distance,
he can see it flow.
His blanket on a branch,
GO BO, GO!

A squirrel in the tree, looks down below, he sees Bo's blanket, and down he goes.

They pull on the blanket,
to and fro,
until it's set free,
to Bo below.

Bo is sleepy,
and it starts to show.
It's time for bed,
GO BO, GO.

www.ingramcontent.com/pod-product-compliance
Lightning Source LLC
Chambersburg PA
CBHW051307110526
44589CB00025B/2966